CRYPTID GUIDES: CREATURES OF FOLKLORE

GUIDE TO ZOMBIES

BY CARRIE GLEASON

CRABTREE
Publishing Company
www.crabtreebooks.com

Developed and produced by Plan B Book Packagers
www.planbbookpackagers.com
Art director: Rosie Gowsell Pattison

Crabtree editor: Ellen Rodger
Crabtree managing editor: Kathy Middleton
Crabtree production coordinator: Katherine Berti
Proofreader: Melissa Boyce

Photographs:
p. 8-9 Rosie Gowsell Pattison. All other photos from Shutterstock.com.

Library and Archives Canada Cataloguing in Publication
Available at the Library and Archives Canada

Library of Congress Cataloging-in-Publication Data
Available at the Library of Congress

Hardcover: 9781039663497   Paperback: 9781039663985
Ebook (pdf): 9781039668416   Epub: 9781039685819

Crabtree Publishing Company
www.crabtreebooks.com   1-800-387-7650

Printed in the U.S.A./072022/CG20220201

Published in Canada
Crabtree Publishing
616 Welland Ave.
St. Catharines, Ontario
L2M 5V6

Published in the United States
Crabtree Publishing
347 Fifth Ave.
Suite 1402-145
New York, NY 10016

CONTENTS

Cryptids and Kinfolk............. 4

Fear the Zombie 6

Anatomy of a Zombie............. 8

Zombies in Action................10

Zombies Around the World... 12

Ghoul vs Zombie 14

Zombie Origins 16

Zonbis Sighted in Haiti! 18

Back From the Dead........... 20

Zombies Make It Big 22

Lifespan of a Zombie........... 24

Surviving the Zombie
Apocalypse...................... 26

Quest for Flesh.................. 28

Zombies Explained.............. 30

Learning More.................... 31

Glossary and Index 32

CRYPTIDS and KINFOLK

This chart shows some of the best-known cryptids and creatures from folklore. How many of them do you think are real?

LAND DWELLER

UNDEAD

LIVING

SPIRIT

LIVING CORPSE

HUMANOID

Zombie

Mummy

Werewolf

Werecat

Grim Reaper

Ghoul

Vampire

Bigfoot

Mothman

WHAT IS A ZOMBIE?

A zombie is a creature from folklore. In folklore there are many different types of creatures that are generally believed to be made up, such as werewolves, vampires, elves, and giants. Other creatures from folklore are cryptids, which are animals that may or may not exist, such as Bigfoot or the Loch Ness Monster. The information on zombies from this book comes from folklore and popular culture. Could zombies be real? This Cryptid Guide will help you decide!

ANIMAL & HYBRID

Unicorn

Jackalope

Chupacabra

OTHERWORLDLY

Fairy

Elf

Nymph

GIANT

Ogre

Troll

EXTRATERRESTRIAL

SEA MONSTER

SWAMP MONSTER

Mermaid

Sea Serpent

LAKE MONSTER

Alien

Louisiana Swamp Monster

Leviathan

Loch Ness Monster

Ogopogo

Champ

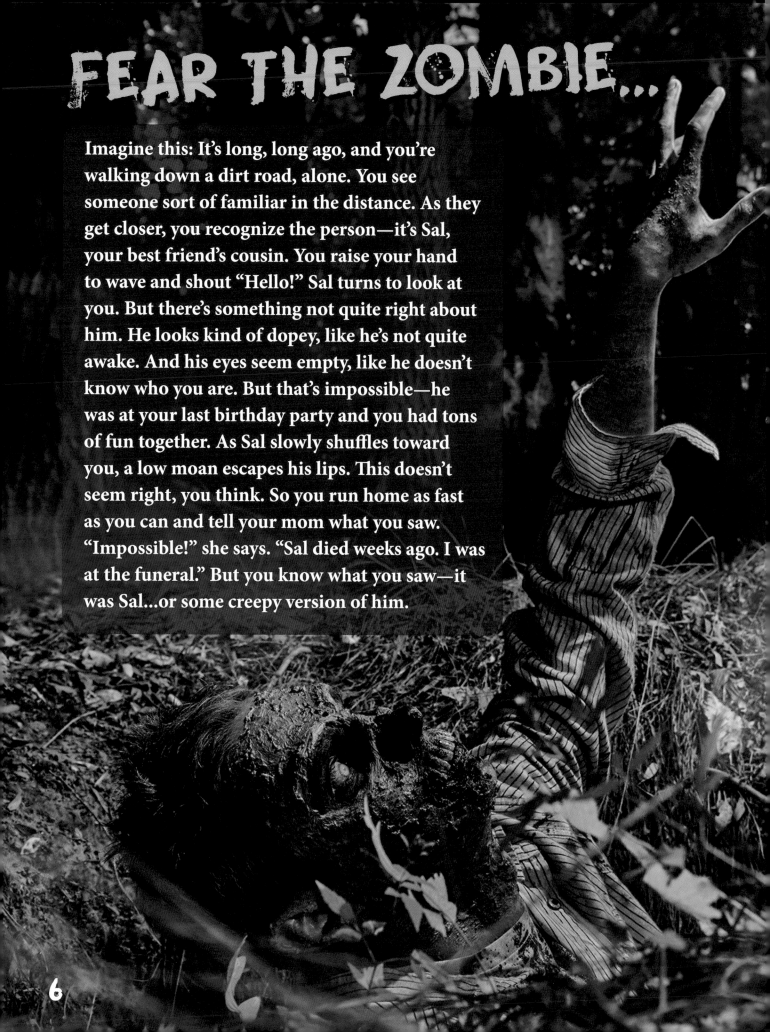

FEAR THE ZOMBIE...

Imagine this: It's long, long ago, and you're walking down a dirt road, alone. You see someone sort of familiar in the distance. As they get closer, you recognize the person—it's Sal, your best friend's cousin. You raise your hand to wave and shout "Hello!" Sal turns to look at you. But there's something not quite right about him. He looks kind of dopey, like he's not quite awake. And his eyes seem empty, like he doesn't know who you are. But that's impossible—he was at your last birthday party and you had tons of fun together. As Sal slowly shuffles toward you, a low moan escapes his lips. This doesn't seem right, you think. So you run home as fast as you can and tell your mom what you saw. "Impossible!" she says. "Sal died weeks ago. I was at the funeral." But you know what you saw—it was Sal...or some creepy version of him.

ZOMBIE BASICS

According to folklore, zombies are people that have been brought back from the dead. They may look human, but they are not to be confused with the person they used to be. These creatures are zoned-out, rotting corpses that crave human flesh. The idea of zombies comes from the Caribbean country of Haiti. There, "zonbis" were people who were cursed and enslaved by a cruel, witch-like creature called a bocor. Over time the legends of zombies have evolved, thanks to popular movies, books, and TV shows. Today's zombies infect people with a zombie virus by biting them, and they have a hankering for human brains. For all their faults, however, they are one of our most beloved monsters.

FAMOUS MONSTERS

Mummy

A mummy is a dead human whose muscles and organs have been preserved rather than left to rot. Real mummies are found in Egypt and South America. Reanimated mummies and their cursed tombs are the stuff of folklore.

Swamp Monster

A swamp monster is a living creature from folklore that makes its home in swamps and other murky waters. Swamp monsters come in many different forms, from humanoid lizards to aquatic plant-covered blobs.

Werewolf

Werewolves come from European folklore. They are living people that transform into wolf form during a full moon. Werewolves are known to attack and kill animals and humans.

ANATOMY OF A ZOMBIE

A dead body decomposes, or rots, over time. The soft tissue (such as skin, organs, and muscle) decays when tiny living things called microorganisms grow on the corpse.

Zombies—they're mindless, moaning horrors known for their never-ending hunger for human flesh. A zombie is a dead body that lacks a soul or spirit but can still move around. Here's how to spot a zombie.

Not that smart, most of its thinking is about finding food

Has a very strong odor of rotting flesh

Makes sounds like labored breathing

Has keen senses of hearing and smell

Eyes look empty or dead

Blackened teeth from lack of brushing

EAT OR BE EATEN

We could say that zombies are good for the environment because they play a role in helping recycle nutrients. Here's how they might fit into nature's nutrient cycle.

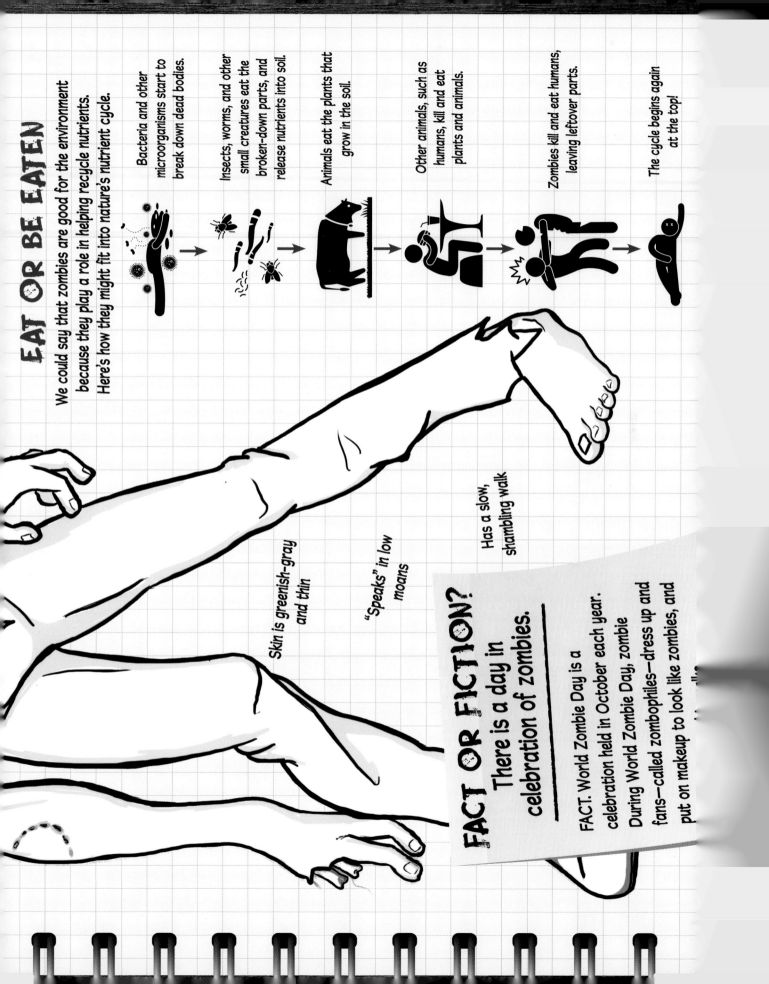

Bacteria and other microorganisms start to break down dead bodies.

Insects, worms, and other small creatures eat the broken-down parts, and release nutrients into soil.

Animals eat the plants that grow in the soil.

Other animals, such as humans, kill and eat plants and animals.

Zombies kill and eat humans, leaving leftover parts.

The cycle begins again at the top!

Skin is greenish-gray and thin

"Speaks" in low moans

Has a slow, shambling walk

FACT OR FICTION?
There is a day in celebration of zombies.

FACT. World Zombie Day is a celebration held in October each year. During World Zombie Day, zombie fans—called zombophiles—dress up and put on makeup to look like zombies, and

ZOMBIES IN ACTION

You might think that a zombie has just one goal—to devour human flesh. But whether they know it or not, some zombies' main purpose is to infect the living with a zombie virus. Zombies aren't very social creatures (since their personalities died when they did), but they often roam together in groups called a herd, a horde, or a swarm.

TYPES OF ZOMBIES

DANGER METER

CRAWLERS

Missing one or both legs, usually because they have rotted off. Don't underestimate them, they can launch into the air using what's left of their upper-body muscles.

DANGER METER

WALKERS

Your everyday zombie, just wandering around looking for someone to bite.

If you don't want to go looking for a zombie, you can wait for someone you know to turn into one.

SOMEONE MIGHT BE A ZOMBIE IF...

- they never feel pain
- they seem not to recognize people they should know
- they never go to sleep, but don't seem to be fully awake either
- they spend all their time aimlessly ambling around
- they're not grossed out by eating rotting animal organs, such as the liver or brain
- they prefer the taste of human flesh to animal flesh
- they sometimes leave body parts laying around—their own or those of others

SOMEONE MIGHT BECOME A ZOMBIE IF...

- they are cursed or forced to drink a zombie potion
- they are infected by a zombie virus (for which there is no known cure)

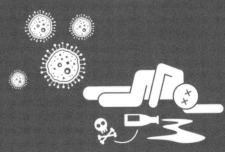

RUNNERS

Fast, like super fast. And smart.

SPITTERS AND PUKERS

These zombies don't bite. They infect the living with a deadly zombie virus that is spewed from their mouths from a medium distance away.

DANGER METER

EXPLODERS

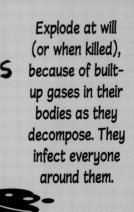

Explode at will (or when killed), because of built-up gases in their bodies as they decompose. They infect everyone around them.

ZOMBIES AROUND THE WORLD

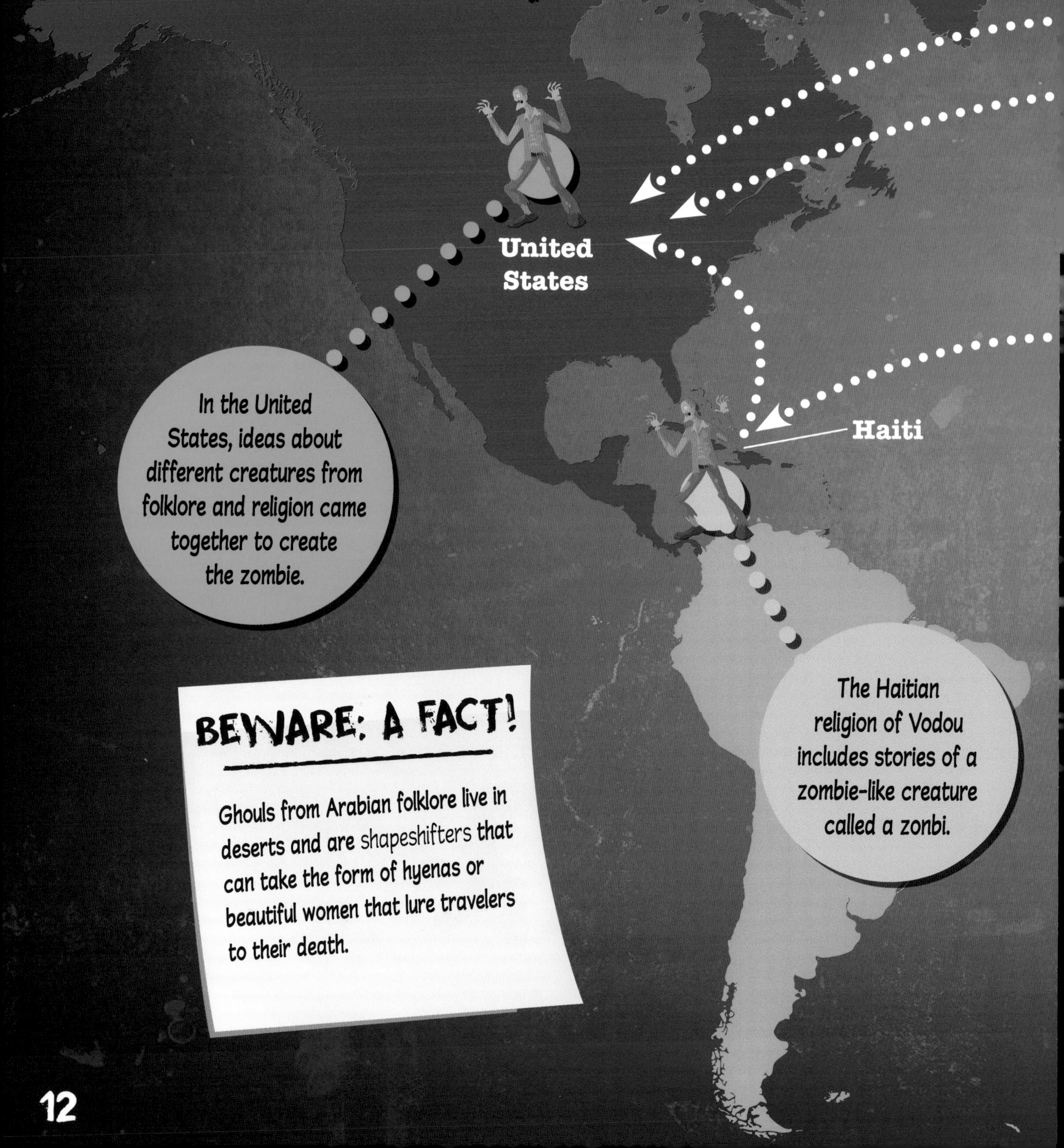

United States

Haiti

In the United States, ideas about different creatures from folklore and religion came together to create the zombie.

BEWARE: A FACT!

Ghouls from Arabian folklore live in deserts and are shapeshifters that can take the form of hyenas or beautiful women that lure travelers to their death.

The Haitian religion of Vodou includes stories of a zombie-like creature called a zonbi.

The idea that zombies can infect people they bite with a virus was borrowed from vampire folklore from Europe.

Zombies are much like ghouls, which originated in Arabian tales. These tales spread to Europe before reaching the United States.

Vodou shares many similarities with the religion of Vodun from West Africa.

Europe

Arabia

Africa

ZOMBIE HODGEPODGE

Zombies are a mixture of creatures from folklore in different parts of the world. Their appearance and behavior was borrowed from creatures from Arabia, Europe, and the Caribbean before becoming the modern zombie we know today from movies made in the United States.

GHOUL VS ZOMBIE

Before there were zombies, there were ghouls. A ghoul is any type of undead creature that feeds on human flesh, so a zombie could be considered a type of ghoul. See how zombies and ghouls compare with these ten facts.

1

Breathing
A zombie is a rotting corpse, whereas a ghoul is not. Neither ghouls nor zombies breathe air.

GHOUL

2

Life
Ghouls are humanoid demons. Zombies were once living humans.

3

Smarts
Ghouls are more clever and devious than zombies.

4

Eyes
A ghoul's eyes are a yellow color. A zombie's eyes are void, or empty of life, and the same color they were when it was alive.

5

Appearance
Both ghouls and zombies have gray skin, but a ghoul's may be more blue-tinged and a zombie's more green-tinged.

6

Cemeteries
Both ghouls and zombies can be found around cemeteries. Ghouls make their homes in cemeteries, where they feed on the newly dead, whereas zombies tend to feed on the living.

ZOMBIE

Ghouls were introduced to Europe in the early 1700s when *One Thousand and One Nights* was translated from the Arabic language into French. The translator, Antoine Galland, added the idea that ghouls dig up graves and eat corpses!

8

Light

Ghouls are creatures of the darkness and they cannot stand sunlight or artificial light, as it affects their speed and strength. Zombies are active day and night.

9

Communication

Ghouls make hissing or growling sounds. Zombies make moaning sounds.

7

Pain

Neither ghouls nor zombies feel pain and both can withstand serious wounds. Neither can be poisoned.

10

Features

A ghoul has a gaunt face, a large mouth filled with tiny sharp teeth, long thin arms, and clawed hands. A zombie's features are similar to living humans' features, but in various stages of decomposition.

15

ZOMBIE ORIGINS

What could be worse than being eaten by a zombie? For the people who follow the Vodou religion, becoming a zombie is a fate far worse. The "zonbi" from the Haitian Vodou religion is not a flesh-eating monster, but a person whose soul has been captured and enslaved.

The Vodou religion comes from the Caribbean country of Haiti. It developed from a mix of the beliefs of West African peoples enslaved on French plantations and Christianity forced upon them by the plantation owners. Vodou was introduced to other countries of the Caribbean and to the United States, especially the state of Louisiana, through the slave trade.

In Vodou beliefs, a person has two types of souls, one which makes the person who they are, and the other that gives them life. A type of witch or sorcerer called a bocor can use a combination of curses and potions to separate a person's soul from their physical body and life force. When this happens, the person has "died" and can be controlled as a living, breathing corpse—minus its soul. Called a "zonbi," this being is enslaved by the bocor.

SLAVERY

Enslaved people in Haiti were denied their free will and their individuality. They were forced to work under harsh conditions and were beaten if they refused. For some, death meant an escape from slavery. The fear of being enslaved even after death—for themselves or their loved ones—was terrifying. To prevent a loved one from becoming a zonbi, people were buried under heavy stones so that their corpses could not rise from the dead, and their graves were watched over for a time after burial.

GUEDE

A zonbi can be turned back into a human by a spirit called a guede. A guede is a healer that is often shown dressed like an undertaker.

FACT OR FICTION?

It is illegal to turn a person into a zombie in Haiti.

FACT. Some people think that Article 246 of Haiti's criminal code means that it is illegal to turn someone into a zombie. Simply put, the law states that it is a crime of murder to give a person zombie powder, even if they do walk again as the undead!

THE CRYPTID RECORD

Cryptozoology's #1 Source for Sightings

Zonbis Sighted in Haiti!

Researcher Tries to Solve Zombie Powder Mystery, 1982

Canadian researcher Wade Davis arrived in Haiti to try and uncover the secret of how bocors make zombie powder. He met with Vodou practitioners and studied the local plants and animals. His theory was that a potion could make it seem like a person had died even though they were still alive. The most likely ingredient, Davis believed, was tetrodotoxin—a toxic substance found naturally in some animals, such as pufferfish. It causes a person to become paralyzed and their breathing to slow down.

Reported Sightings

There have been numerous real reports of people who have been turned into Haitian zonbis. In most cases the individuals had been reported dead only to resurface years later. The stories on these pages are based on real reports.

Police Befuddled
1980

The police officer who declared Natagette Joseph deceased in 1966 got a surprise when he spotted the woman wandering around the village. The officer, although not a doctor, was certain he was not mistaken all those years ago when he pronounced her dead. The only explanation, he claimed, was zombiism.

Fingerprints Confirm Zonbi Returns
1981

Fingerprint experts agreed that Clairvius Narcisse was who he claimed to be. The man, who died in Schweitzer Hospital in 1963, returned to his village claiming that he had been under the control of a bocor.

Grave Opened
1979

Three years after Francina Illeus was pronounced dead and buried, she was found in a confused state in a market. Her mother knew it was her because she recognized the scar on her forehead. When officials reopened Francina's grave they found it contained only rocks.

Bocor Strikes Again!
1936

Twenty-nine years after her death, a woman claiming to be Felicia Flix-Mentor was found walking on a country road. Strangely, the woman had no eyelashes and was wearing no clothing except for a piece of cloth wrapped around her head. Her family, including her brother, son, and husband, were called upon to prove her identity. The woman was very confused and remained in hospital for some time.

BACK FROM THE DEAD

Another word for a creature that is undead or that has returned from the dead is a revenant. Zombies, vampires, and ghosts are all revenants. Revenants can be broken into two groups: corporeal and spirit.

Corporeal vs Spirit

Corporeal revenants are reanimated corpses, or dead bodies that are brought back to life. The soul, or spirit, does not return, which means they are not the same person that they were when alive.

Spirit revenants do not have a physical body, although they may have a physical shape. Another way of putting it is that they are the bodiless souls of people who were once alive.

VAMPIRES

Vampires are undead creatures from Eastern European folklore. Vampires were once humans who awoke after death with a thirst for human blood.

20

SPIRIT

GHOSTS

Ghosts are the spirits of people who have died. Ghosts can be transparent, shadowy figures, human-like figures, whiffs of smoke or fog, or a form of light. Ghosts are said to haunt places that were special to them in life.

CORPOREAL

DRAUGRS

Draugrs come from Norse folklore and legends. They are found around their graves protecting the treasures they were buried with. Draugrs have some special powers, such as the ability to shapeshift and enter the dreams of the living.

CORPOREAL

NACHZEHRER

A nachzehrer comes from German folklore. It is a cross between a vampire and a ghoul that returns from the dead. A nachzehrer feasts on human flesh or energy for nine years after its death.

SPIRIT

WRAITHS

A wraith comes from Scottish folklore. It is the spirit of a dying person that leaves the body and appears just before, during, and after the time of death. Wraiths do not cause harm.

ZOMBIES MAKE IT BIG

Zombie bodies may be decaying, but their popularity is not! Zombies are the stars of horror movies, comics, books, and video games. But instead of flesh-eating monsters, zombies today are also sometimes shown as love interests, friends, and creatures to be pitied. This timeline gives you an idea of how zombies have changed over time.

1968
Night of the Living Dead, George A. Romero's first zombie horror movie, is released. It was inspired by a vampire story. Romero referred to his monsters as a type of ghoul.

1940
Weird Tales magazine publishes a story called "Song of the Slaves" about a plantation owner who murders enslaved Africans. They return from the dead to seek revenge.

1985
In the film *The Return of the Living Dead* the zombies eat brains for the first time.

1998
The children's movie *Scooby-Doo on Zombie Island* is released. Unlike other Scooby-Doo shows, where the monsters end up being people in costumes, the zombies are real.

2018
Zombies sing and dance in the musical teen movie *Zombies,* featuring pale, green-haired zombies in high school. The movie is based on the book *Zombies & Cheerleaders.*

2011
Zombie characters are added to the video game *Minecraft.* They are slow-moving, but can attack together in hordes, or groups.

START HERE

1929
The Magic Island by W.B. Seabrook is published. The book, about Seabrook's travels in Haiti, describes corpses brought back to life and enslaved.

1932
A story called "The House in the Magnolias" is published. It is about a man who finds a plantation with zombies in New Orleans. The zombies are freed from their curse by giving them salt.

1932
White Zombie, a film based on the ideas from Seabrook's book, is released. In it, a woman is turned into a zombie by an evil "voodoo" master while visiting a plantation in Haiti.

2002
In the post-apocalyptic movie *28 Days Later*, a zombie virus has taken over and zombies become scarier because they are fast-moving.

2004
Zombies get funny in the British-made comedy-horror movie *Shaun of the Dead*.

2010
The TV show *The Walking Dead* airs. It follows a small group of people who survived a zombie apocalypse. The only way to kill the zombies, called "walkers," is to destroy their brains or burn them.

2005
The first issue in the *Marvel Zombies* comics series is released, in which popular Marvel characters such as the Hulk and Wolverine have been infected by a zombie virus.

LIFESPAN OF A ZOMBIE

A single zombie only "lives" for about five weeks. It's important that a zombie is caught right away, before it can infect others. A zombie outbreak occurs when there are a few cases of zombie infection in a certain area. If it is not stopped, it grows into an epidemic, which means the virus has spread to multiple places. Worst of all is a zombie pandemic—this is when the virus has spread to multiple countries or continents, or even the entire world! This timeline shows what happens to a zombie's body in its short life.

It would take 20 days for the first zombie to start a zombie epidemic. By day 100, there would only be 273 people left alive on the planet!

Age: 24–72 hours old

There is little change in the way a zombie looks from when it was alive. The tendons and muscles stiffen (called rigor mortis), and bacteria eat up any remaining oxygen in the body. Insects begin to lay eggs on the corpse.

Age: 4–10 days old

The body starts to decay. Bacteria in the digestive tract produce smelly gases and make the body puffy, or bloated. Skin looks greenish. Escaping gases from inside the body cause skin to crack open.

Age: 11–25 days old

Maggots and insects move in, breaking down the body even more by feeding on soft tissue. Liquid from inside the body oozes out. Body odor is very strong.

Age: 26–50 days old

Bones have become exposed and there is hardly any soft tissue left. Even maggots don't want much to do with a zombie at this age.

Dead again!

After about 50 days, there is nothing left to hold the zombie's bones and teeth in place and it will simply fall apart!

SURVIVING THE ZOMBIE APOCALYPSE

It's happened—a zombie pandemic. The world is overrun by zombies and the zombie apocalypse is upon us. There is no electricity and no Internet. All of the things that make our lives comfortable are gone, and your life is in danger. How will you survive?

SURVIVAL 101
STEP 1: GATHER SUPPLIES, YOU WILL NEED...

- enough food to last until all the zombies have rotted away
- candles or other soft light, such as flashlights or glowsticks
- salt
- a sword-like weapon (even a shovel will do)
- first-aid supplies
- water

TIP: Pack plant-based foods. Zombies prefer fresh flesh, but you don't want to risk attracting one by frying up a burger!

STEP 2: FIND SHELTER AND ZOMBIE-PROOF IT

- Board up all windows and barricade doors by piling extra furniture in front of them (zombies can be strong).
- Turn off all phones and alarms. Zombies will be attracted by the noise they make and come to investigate.
- Turn off all the lights at night.
- Keep everyone together in one room—that way you can make sure no one has been turned into a zombie when you weren't looking.

TIP: Zombies are afraid of fire and are startled by sudden loud noises. In the event of a zombie breach, you can try making a quick getaway by setting off firecrackers.

STEP 3: KNOW HOW TO STOP A ZOMBIE

- Destroy its brain.
- Chop off its head. (Beware: the head will continue to exist on its own—but it can't move around to catch you.)
- Feed it salt. Some legends say that salt will cause all of a zombie's fluids to drain from its body, killing it.

TIP: Poison has no effect on zombies.

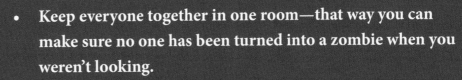

QUEST FOR FLESH

Zombies aren't the only ones on the hunt for human flesh. It may be hard to believe today, but some humans in history also ate human flesh. Humans eating other humans' flesh or body parts is called cannibalism.

HUMAN CANNIBALS

Cannibalism was not uncommon in different parts of the world throughout history. Sometimes these acts were done as part of religious rituals or during times when people were starving. Other times, certain body parts were used to make medicine. In Europe in the 1500s to 1700s, for example, a powder made from ground-up mummies was used in medicine. And if no mummies were available, people got the ingredients from recently deceased criminals!

ROBBING GRAVES—FOR SCIENCE!

The story of Frankenstein's monster may seem like make-believe to us now, but it is based on real experiments done in the 1800s to try and reanimate corpses, or bring them back to life. Sometimes the body parts needed for these experiments came from grave robbers, who dug up freshly buried bodies at night. Grave robbers also sold bodies to medical schools so that students training to be doctors could use them to practice on!

BURIED ALIVE

There have been real cases in history where people were buried alive! The fear of being buried alive is called taphephobia. John G. Krichbaum, an inventor from Youngstown, Ohio, came up with a solution for it. In 1882 he invented the "Device for Indicating Life in Buried Persons." It was made up of two pipes, one inside the other, that go from the inside of a coffin to the surface. If the buried person woke up, they could simply move a lever that would make the inner pipe pop up. The pipe also allowed oxygen into the coffin so the person could survive until rescued.

Zombies Explained

There are a few medical conditions that may cause people to act or look like zombies—minus the eating of human flesh, of course!

Catatonia

Catatonia is a medical condition in which people seem to be in a stupor, or nearly **unconscious** state. It is rare but can be found in people who have mood disorders or a disease called Parkinson's. People who are catatonic usually don't speak or respond to what's going on around them. They also stare blankly, hold their bodies in unusual poses, and seem to wander around aimlessly.

Bacterial infections

Certain bacterial skin infections can make people look like their skin is rotting. People with a skin infection called yaws have open sores all over their body, joint stiffness, and feel very tired all the time. Flesh-eating disease is another example of a bacterial infection. It causes death in parts of the body's soft tissue and is extremely painful.

Cotard's syndrome

People that have a rare **psychiatric** condition called Cotard's syndrome believe that they are rotting or have lost body parts—or even their souls!

Zombie Animals

In nature, zombie animals are animals that have been infected by certain types of parasites that take over the animals' minds and bodies and control their behavior. The animals below have all been known to turn into zombie animals when infected.

Zombie ant

Zombie caterpillar

Zombie bee

Zombie stick inse

Zombie crab

LEARNING MORE

Want to know more about cryptids, myths, and monsters such as the ones described in this book? Here are some resources to check out while on your cryptid-hunting quest.

Books

Behind the Legend: Zombies by Erin Peabody. Little Bee Books, 2017.

Monster Science: Could Monsters Survive (and Thrive!) in the Real World? by Helaine Becker. Kids Can Press, 2016.

The Last Kids on Earth and the Zombie Parade by Max Brallier. Viking Books, 2016.

TV and Films

Monstrum is a series of videos created by PBS about monsters, myths, and legends.

Find the videos on the PBS website at:

www.pbs.org/show/monstrum/

Websites

The Centre for Fortean Zoology is a cryptozoology organization that researches cryptids from around the world. They produce a weekly TV show, books, and magazines about cryptids.

www.cfz.org.uk/

GLOSSARY

apocalypse A disastrous event that leads to the end of the world as we know it

corpse A dead body

digestive tract A tube-shaped passageway in the body that leads from the mouth to the bum

enslave To take away someone's freedom and treat them as your property

folklore The stories, customs, and beliefs that people of a certain place share and pass down through the generations

humanoid Something that is not human but has the appearance or behavior of one

infect To spread germs or disease to someone

maggot The larva of an insect, usually a fly

paralyzed Unable to move

parasite A living thing that lives in or on another living thing and robs it of nutrients to survive

plantation A large farm that grows one main crop

popular culture The movies, music, TV, books, and fashion that everyone is interested in at a certain time

preserve To keep fresh; the opposite of rot

psychiatric Relating to mental or emotional health in people

reanimated Brought back to life

religious ritual A set of actions that people do during spiritual worship

shapeshifter A creature that has the ability to take a different form or shape

slave trade The capturing, selling, and buying of enslaved people

tendon A tissue in the body that attaches muscle to bone

unconscious A very deep, sleep-like state

virus Tiny germs that infect the cells of the body, where they reproduce and spread

INDEX

bacteria 9, 24, 30
bocors 7, 16, 18, 19
body parts 7, 8, 10, 11, 25, 28, 30
brains 7, 11, 22, 23, 27
burials 17, 21, 28, 29
cannibalism 28
catatonia 30
cemeteries 14
curses 6, 11, 16, 22
Davis, Wade 19
decomposition 8, 9, 11, 15, 24-25, 27, 30
diseases 30
draugrs 21

epidemic 24
eyes 6, 8, 14
fire 23, 27
Flix-Mentor, Felicia 19
ghosts 4, 21
ghouls 4, 12, 13, 14-15, 21, 22
grave robbers 28
guede 17
Haiti 7, 12, 16-17, 18-19, 23
horde 10, 22
Illeus, Francina 19
Joseph, Natagette 19
laws 17
lifespan 24-25

maggots 25
mummies 4, 7, 28
mummy powder 28
nachzehrer 21
Narcisse, Clairvius 19
odor 8, 25
outbreak 24
pandemic 24, 26
religion 12, 13, 16, 18
revenants 20-21
salt 23, 27
skin 8, 9, 14, 24, 30
slavery 7, 16-17
soul (or spirit) 8, 16, 20-21,

30
swamp monsters 5, 7
vampires 4, 5, 13, 20, 21, 22
viruses 7, 10-11, 13, 23, 24
werewolves 4, 5, 7
World Zombie Day 9
wraiths 21
zombie animals 30
zombie potions 11, 1
zombie powder 17,
zombie types 10-1
zombie walks 9
zombophiles 9
zonbi 7, 12, 16